Sharing Blessings

CHILDREN'S STORIES FOR EXPLORING THE SPIRIT OF THE JEWISH HOLIDAYS

by Rahel Musleah and Rabbi Michael Klayman

Illustrated by Mary O'Keefe Young

Jewish Lights Publishing

Woodstock, Vermont

To Shira and Shoshana, our shared blessings.

Acknowledgments

To Stuart Matlins: You encouraged our vision; Sandra Korinchak: Your support, professionalism and caring manner made the publishing process a pleasure; Amy Gottlieb: Your creative suggestions and keen insights helped give this book its shape and style; Dr. Ron Wolfson and David and Shira Milgrom-Elcott: You inspired the Passover chapter.

To Michael's parents, Rhoda and Bob Klayman: Had you had the opportunity to see this book, how proud you would be!

To Rahel's parents, Rabbi Ezekiel and Margaret Musleah: You taught us the power of blessings and shared your love for the richness of the holidays.

To all the children and adults who have celebrated Jewish life with us: A part of each of you is in this book.

Sharing Blessings:
Children's Stories for Exploring the Spirit of the Jewish Holidays
Text © 1997 by Rahel Musleah and Michael Klayman
Illustrations © 1997 by Mary O'Keefe Young

Musleah, Rahel.
Sharing blessings : children's stories for exploring the spirit of the Jewish holidays / by Rahel Musleah and Michael Klayman ; illustrated by Mary O'Keefe Young.
      p.   cm.

Summary: Explores the spiritual meaning of each of thirteen Jewish holidays and suggests ways to make these feasts an important part of everyday life.

ISBN 1-879045-71-0 (hc)

1. Fasts and feasts—Judaism—Juvenile literature. [1. Fasts and feasts—Judaism. 2. Judaism—Customs and practices.]
I. Klayman, Michael, 1954– . II. Young, Mary O' Keefe, ill. III. Title.
BM690.M87 1997
296.4'3—dc21   96–30047
                                     CIP
                                     AC

10 9 8 7 6 5 4 3 2 1

ISBN 1-879045-71-0 (Hardcover)

Manufactured in the United States of America

Book and jacket designed by Lindy Gifford

Jewish Lights Publishing
A Division of LongHill Partners, Inc.
P.O. Box 237
Sunset Farm Offices, Route 4
Woodstock, Vermont 05091
Tel: (802) 457-4000   Fax (802) 457-4004

1 ✡ Shabbat

Sharing Blessings

Family

Ilana and David Kedner go to school all week. When Shabbat comes, they look forward to a rest! From a few minutes before the sun sets on Friday until Ilana and David can see three stars in the sky on Saturday night, they know it's Shabbat. The Kedners love the Shabbat traditions. Mom lights two candles to welcome Shabbat. Over a cup of wine, the family recites *kiddush*, the blessing that makes the day holy and special. They say *motzi*, the blessing over the braided challah bread. Between *kiddush* and *motzi*, Mom and Dad bless Ilana and David. Then it's time for a delicious Shabbat meal.

Sometimes the Kedners go to the synagogue on Friday night. Often, they attend services on Shabbat morning to sing the prayers and hear the Torah being read. They greet friends by saying *Shabbat Shalom!* Have a peaceful Shabbat! Ilana, David and their parents say goodbye to Shabbat with a *havdalah* service that separates Shabbat from the rest of the week. They light a tall, braided *havdalah* candle, make a blessing over wine and sniff spices like cloves and cinnamon. They hope the light and sweetness of Shabbat will last all week.

The kitchen always felt different on Friday afternoon before Shabbat. Ilana couldn't quite put her finger on it. Maybe it was the way the air felt sweet. Not sticky sweet like caramel or maple syrup or fudge, but sweet from the warmth of freshly baked challah and her mother's smile as she stirred the soup. Or maybe it was the spicy smell of the Indian vegetable curry and rice Mom loved or the aroma of Ilana's favorite carrot pudding. Mom usually didn't have time to cook like that during the week.

Mom lifted a tray out of the oven. On it were two beautiful, brown, baked-to-the crisp challahs, so fragrant with yeast and eggs and honey that Ilana felt as if she were smelling them for the first time. She knew they would be white and fluffy inside.

Dad was already setting the table in the dining room. "I could use some help in here," he called. Ilana and David got up reluctantly. "Your enthusiasm is contagious," Dad chuckled.

Ilana draped a lace lavender cloth over the white one that was already on the table. She set two extra places for Grandma and Grandpa, who were coming for dinner. David put out the colorful pottery challah tray from Jerusalem, decorated with a bright border of painted flowers. Ilana added the kiddush cups made from delicate blue glass that Mom and Dad had bought in Italy.

Soon the sun began to set. Mom waited for David and Ilana to change into clean, comfortable clothes before she lit the Shabbat candles. The two sturdy white candles in their silver holders always reminded Ilana of a pair of doves waiting to open the Shabbat gates. Mom lit the candles, closed her eyes and recited the blessing. Dad, Ilana and David stood behind her. Ilana gazed at the flames shimmering softly. Shabbat had begun.

David flew to answer a loud knock on the door. "Grandma! Grandpa!" He leapt into his grandparents' arms and pulled them both into the dining room.

"Careful, bubbaleh," Grandma said, cradling a shopping bag. "You'll squash the chocolate chip cookies."

The family gathered around the table. Ilana swayed as they sang *Shalom Aleikhem* and recited the kiddush over the wine to welcome Shabbat. David marched in a circle like a robot.

Ilana ran to Dad. "Time for my *berachah*." She bent her head to receive the Shabbat blessing. Dad put his hands gently on her head. She liked being so close to him that she could see each hair of the graying stubble on his cheek. He was wearing the watch she and David had bought him for Father's Day.

"May God bless you with the blessings of Sarah, Rebecca, Rachel and Leah," he said, kissing her on the cheek. She hugged him.

"Time for your *berachah*," Mom called David. Still pretending to be a robot, he walked to her in stiff slow motion. Mom put her hands on his head and recited the words of Jacob's blessing to his grandchildren.

"May God bless you with the blessings of Ephraim and Menasseh." She kissed David on the cheek and he squirmed and tried to wriggle away. "Whoever heard of a robot being blessed," he frowned.

Mom continued the blessing in a deep, staccato, robot-like voice: "May-God-bless-you-and-guard-you." David smiled.

Dad finished the blessing. "May God show you favor and be gracious to you. May God show you kindness and grant you peace." Ilana and David sat down.

"It's time for my *berachah* from Grandma and Grandpa." Mom stood up.

"You're too old for a *berachah*," David giggled. "That's only for kids."

"You say that every time Grandma and Grandpa spend Shabbat with us," Ilana answered.

"No matter how old your Mom is," Grandma turned to David, "she's still our child. And your dad is like our child also."

"You should have seen your mom as a six-year-old," Grandpa winked. "Was she ever cute!"

"Were you a pest like David, Mom?" Ilana teased.

"Mom! Tell her to stop!" David cried. "She's so mean!"

"Try not to argue on Shabbat," Dad sighed.

"Why do you want me to be like Sarah, Rebecca, Rachel and Leah, who lived so long ago?" Ilana asked.

"That's a good question, Ilana," Mom said. "Here's an idea. Pretend we were living in ancient Israel. Our tent is all ready for Shabbat."

"I don't think they had braided challah back then," Ilana said. "I'll put some fresh pita bread on the table. Then I'll change into my best robe, the one I wove from scarlet wool."

"My pet camel Gamliel is already resting outside," David added.

"When Shabbat begins, we bless you as our mothers and fathers blessed us," Dad said, "with the blessings of Sarah, Rebecca, Rachel and Leah, Ephraim and Menasseh—people who were wise, strong and faithful to God."

"I'd like to go back to Spain," Grandpa said. "The year is 1482. It's Friday night. The candles in the corner shed the only light in the dark room where we are welcoming Shabbat in secret. The curtains are drawn so no one will see what we're doing or discover we're Jewish."

"Why would you want to go to a place like that?" Ilana shuddered.

"Jews in Spain are not allowed to *show* we're Jewish," Grandpa answered. "But being Jewish is so important to us that we are willing to take risks even in dangerous times."

"As Shabbat begins, our children draw near. We whisper the words of the blessing we've heard from our mothers and fathers," Mom said.

"Silently, we add a secret prayer," Dad continued. "We hope that when you are adults and bless your own children, it will be in freedom."

"I get it," David said. "This blessing is really old! Older than you, Grandpa!"

"David!" Mom scolded.

"It's okay," Grandpa laughed. "David got the message. Just as the moms and dads of ancient Israel and 15th-century Spain blessed their children, Grandma and I bless your Mom on Friday night."

"And Mom and Dad bless Ilana and me," David said. "Okay, next time I'm a robot I'll try not to wiggle so much."

"One day I suppose David and I will bless our kids," Ilana giggled.

"Ilana!" David cried. He shook his head. "I'm never going to grow up, so that won't happen to me."

"This blessing has survived no matter when and where Jews have lived, no matter how they lived," Grandpa concluded.

"Before we eat, I have a special blessing this Shabbat for Ilana and David," Grandma said. "And I don't have to say it secretly." She turned to Ilana. "May you be like Sarah, Rebecca, Rachel and Leah, but may you always remain true to Ilana. May you always be thoughtful and creative and generous."

"I like that," David said. "Is it my turn now?"

Grandma smiled at David. "May you be like Ephraim and Menasseh, but may you always remain true to David. May you always be kind and fun and honest."

"And now," Mom smiled, "I'd really, really like my *berachah*!"

May God bless you
with the blessings
of all the mothers and fathers
who came before us,
from Sarah, Rebecca, Rachel and Leah,
from Ephraim and Menasseh,
to our family today.

יְשִׂימֵךְ אֱלֹהִים כְּשָׂרָה, רִבְקָה, רָחֵל וְלֵאָה.

Yesimekh Elohim kearah, rivkah, rachel vele'ah.

יְשִׂימְךָ אֱלֹהִים כְּאֶפְרַיִם וְכִמְנַשֶּׁה.

Yesimekha Elohim ke'efraim vekhimenasheh.

2 ✡ Rosh Hashanah

Being Able to Say "I Did It"

Responsibility

David and Ilana celebrate Rosh Hashanah, the Jewish New Year, on the first and second days of the Hebrew month of Tishrei. Some of their friends only celebrate one day. The holiday begins in the evening with candlelighting, followed by a festive meal. Holiday symbols include a round challah that looks like a crown, reminding us that God rules the world; and apples dipped in honey for a sweet year. David and Ilana greet each other with the words, *Shanah Tovah*— Have a good year! They send cards wishing friends and family a happy new year.

On the afternoon of the first day, David, Ilana and their family gather by a pond, a brook, or any other flowing waters to perform *tashlich*, a ceremony in which they symbolically cast away all their mistakes. Most of all, they look forward to listening to the sound of the *shofar*, the ram's horn, in the synagogue. It wakes them up almost like an alarm clock, stirring them to take responsibility for their mistakes and to act kindly in the year ahead.

Ilana stood at the edge of the duck pond and breathed in the quiet of the early autumn day. It wasn't a perfect afternoon. The clouds hung low in the sky, like a white hammock. Ilana blinked twice as a swan glided past. For a second she thought the swan was a really low cloud that had fallen into the water.

A duck quacked. Ilana peered at it and saw her reflection in the water at the same time. It looked like a blurry photograph. "What will school be like this year?" she wondered. "Who will my friends be? I wish I knew what's ahead."

A shower of pebbles shook the water. Her reflection quivered crazily. Ilana turned around, annoyed. "Hey David, stop that!" she yelled. "You're disturbing the peace."

"It's too quiet!" he yelled back.

"Quiet is good," Ilana said, taking another deep breath. "It helps me think. Life isn't only about action figures and noisy soccer games."

David kicked the grass. "Well, I'm tired of waiting!" he said. "When is the service going to begin? I can't ever remember what it's called."

"*Tashlich*," Ilana answered. "And it's not a service. It's when you take some pebbles, like you just did, or even some dirt or bread crumbs, and throw them into the water. That shows we're getting rid of all the bad things we've done this year. You'd better get a lot of pebbles, David," she grinned.

"You too, Ilana," David shot back. He looked at his shoe. "Oh no!" he cried. "I stepped in something! Mom! Help!"

Mom examined David's shoe and took a tissue out of her pocket. "Life isn't perfect," she laughed. "Somebody always messes up. That's why *tashlich* is so good for us. It helps us to clean up our act."

"Everybody's starting to arrive," Dad said.

"I see Rabbi Aaron and Avi," David pointed. "Why couldn't we just do *tashlich* in synagogue this morning during Rosh Hashanah services?"

"We need flowing water for *tashlich*," Dad explained. "Like the duck pond. And there are different ways of taking responsibility for what we do wrong. One is praying in synagogue. Another is asking the people we hurt to forgive us."

"*Tashlich* is a way of saying, 'I did something wrong,'" Mom said. "Taking responsibility goes beyond words. Because it's hard to change, the pebbles help us get started. We can see them and feel them."

"It's easier to throw pebbles into the water than to actually throw away all the mistakes I've made," Ilana said. A cool breeze shook the trees that bordered the pond. "Maybe I can ask the wind to carry them away."

"Humor me for just a minute," Mom said. "Put some pebbles in your pockets."

Ilana and David stuffed their jacket pockets full of stones. "They're so heavy," David complained.

"I can barely move!" Ilana pretended to stagger.

"Now throw them into the water, one by one," Mom suggested.

David took a fistful of pebbles from his pocket. He threw them in so they would skip across the pond and form circles in the water. "Wow! That last pebble skipped five times. A new personal record!"

Ilana emptied her pockets and paused for a moment before tossing in each pebble. They splashed into the water with a plop, plop, plop plop. When she had thrown in all the pebbles, Ilana sighed. "I feel as light as

a cloud gliding across the sky," she said.

"That's the point," Mom explained. "We're not always aware of our mistakes, but *tashlich* helps us realize how heavy they really are. Like the pebbles, we try to get rid of our mistakes a little at a time. That's an important step in taking responsibility."

"You keep saying that word—responsibility," David said.

"Being responsible means learning to care for something," Mom explained. "Suppose you want to bring your favorite toy to school. Being responsible means making sure you don't lose it or break it."

"Remember when I lost my teddy bear?" David said glumly. "I blamed Avi because he was playing with it."

"Taking responsibility also means being able to say, 'I did it. Not Avi. Not Ilana. Nobody but me.' Otherwise people won't trust you and you won't learn how to be honest," Dad said.

"Before we join everyone for the official *tashlich*, I want to throw in my first pebble," said Mom. "Next time I have a bad day, I'll try not to take my grumpiness out on you." She threw a pebble into the water.

"I'll take responsibility to be around more," Dad said. "Sometimes I just get too busy at work." He threw a pebble into the water.

"Uh oh, David, it's our turn," Ilana said. "We'll try to take responsibility for showing more kindness to each other," she began.

"Yeah," David said. "Instead of yelling and complaining and whining." He dragged a big rock to the water's edge.

"I'll help you, David," Ilana said. She and David pushed the rock into the water. It made such a splash that all the ducks nearby flew away.

"Big changes ahead for all of us!" Dad laughed. "Those ducks are probably heading south early because of us!"

"It's never too early to get a head start," Mom said. "Let's hope the water carries all our pebbles as far as those ducks are flying!"

"But those ducks will be back in the spring," Ilana said. "I hope our mistakes stay away!"

May God help us to rid ourselves of our mistakes and take responsibility for our lives.

וְתַשְׁלִיךְ בִּמְצוֹלוֹת יָם כָּל־חַטֹּאתָם.

Vatashlikh bimtsolot yam kol-chatotam.

3 ✡ Yom Kippur
Talking to God

Prayer

On Yom Kippur, the Day of Atonement, the 10th day of the Hebrew month of Tishrei, Mom and Dad fast. They don't eat or drink for a whole day, so they can concentrate on asking God and each other for forgiveness. Ilana and David don't have to fast because they are children, but they do try to do without sweets or other junk food. That's their way of fasting!

The Kedners spend much of Yom Kippur in the synagogue, praying and accepting responsibility for all the things they are sorry they did during the year. The prayers begin on the eve of Yom Kippur with *Kol Nidrei*, a solemn chant that frees people from promises they have made but were not able to keep. Ilana and her mom like to wear white clothes on Yom Kippur to start the year in a pure, fresh way. David and his dad wear white shirts. When the *shofar*, the ram's horn, is blown at the end of Yom Kippur, the fast is over. Everyone goes home and eats!

David lay in bed on his stomach and shuffled his baseball cards in his hands. The house was so quiet at night. He could hear the steps creak when Dad went downstairs. He pulled his quilt over his head, imagining he was at a baseball game. At Yankee Stadium there would be crowds yelling. Balls cracking against bats. People walking up and down the bleachers calling, "Popcorn!" "Peanuts!" "Ice cream!"

He shifted onto his side and peeked out from under the quilt. The night light threw a shadow on the wall and it was shaped like a glowing circle. David wondered if it was hot to touch. It did look a little fiery. They'd had a fire drill in school today. He clutched his baseball cards so tightly that they squeezed out of his hands and fell onto the floor.

"Mom, Dad," David called. He grabbed his teddy bear.

Dad peered into David's room and sighed. "David, this is the third time you've called. Now what is it?"

"My baseball cards fell on the floor. Can't you stay with me for a few minutes?"

"The lights are out," Dad said firmly. "Sleeping is something you have to do alone. Besides, you need your sleep. We'll be at the synagogue late tomorrow night. It's Yom Kippur."

David burrowed into his quilt again and pulled it over his head. "What's wrong?" Dad asked.

"I don't want to tell you," David mumbled.

"Okay, tell your pillow," Dad said.

David poked his head out and turned to his pillow. "I can't sleep. And I don't like the quiet. It makes me think of all kinds of things, like what would happen if there was a fire in the house."

"Oh, David," Dad stroked his hair. "You never have to be afraid to tell me what's bothering you."

"I was embarrassed," David mumbled again. "Sometimes it's hard to tell anyone what's wrong—even you or Mom."

"Maybe there's someone else you can tell," Dad suggested.

"Not Ilana!" David bolted upright.

"No, I wasn't thinking of Ilana," Dad smiled. "I'll give you a hint. It has to do with Yom Kippur."

"Is it the rabbi?" David asked.

"Sure, the rabbi's a good listener. Who else can you think of?"

"How about God?"

Dad nodded. "That's who I talk to when I'm not sure anyone else will listen or when I can't put into words exactly how I feel. It's called praying."

"Once I prayed to God for a kitten but I didn't get one," David said. "So I didn't think it helped."

"Once I prayed to God to let my dad—your other Grandpa—get better," Dad said. "But he didn't. He died. Praying to God isn't always about God answering. It's about God listening. It's painful not to get the answer you hope for, but it's comforting to know someone is always listening. God is never too busy fixing the car, working at the computer or cooking dinner."

"Yeah. Imagine if God said 'Sorry, I'm fixing the sky. It's leaking,'" David laughed. "Or, 'Sorry, the birds are calling me. I can't listen to you right now.'"

"Praying is something people need," Dad added. "On Yom Kippur we tell God everything we've done wrong so we can try to change. If we were

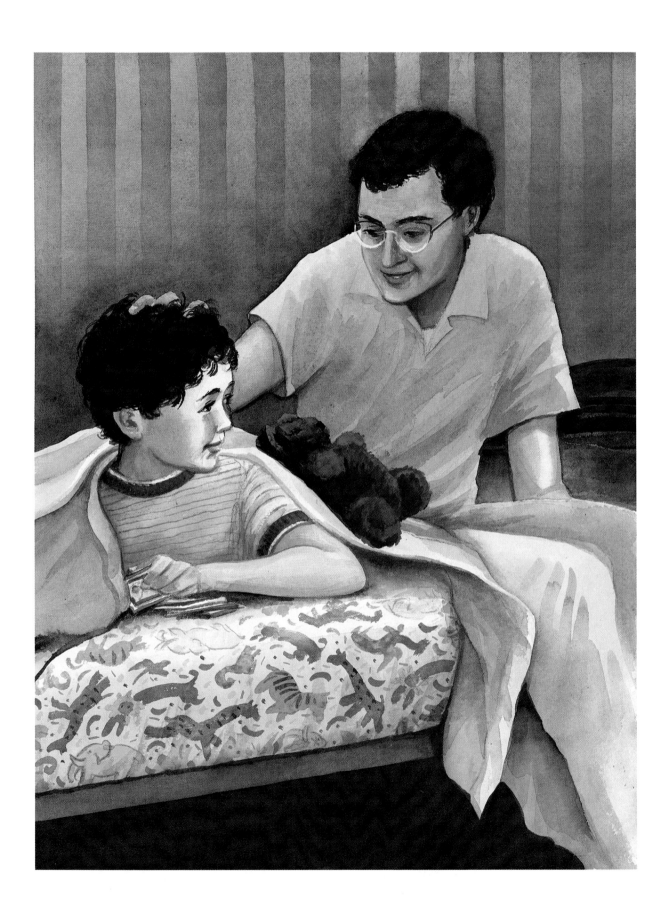

kinder to each other, the world would be a better place."

"Could I say stuff like, 'Sorry, God, I tattled on Ilana. Sorry, God, I ate a whole chocolate bar without eating dinner first.'" David cuddled his teddy bear. "Sorry, Teddy, for when I threw you down the stairs." David looked sadly at Dad. "I sure have a lot of sorries to say. I must have really been bad this year."

"Everyone does things they are sorry for, David. That's what makes us human."

"What are you sorry for, Dad?" David asked.

Dad rubbed his fingers in a circle against his cheek as he thought. "I'm sorry for the times I got angry when I should have listened to you more carefully, and for the times I was so busy watching football that I didn't help Mom enough."

"Once I said Ilana broke a glass when it was my fault," David said. "Won't God be angry with me for that?"

"Did you apologize to Ilana?"

David shook his head.

"Yom Kippur is a good time to say you're sorry for the things you never admitted. That helps us to be wiser and more honest. Only you can apologize to Ilana for hurting her. Like sleeping, you have to do it alone."

"Okay," David groaned. "I'll tell her right now!"

"Silly," Dad tousled David's hair. "If you've waited all this time, you can wait until morning."

"The way you describe it, Dad, praying sounds just like talking," David said. "But in synagogue, I don't understand most of the words."

"That will take time to learn," Dad said. "Until then, you can make up your own words."

"We learned about haiku in school. Can I pray in haiku?"

"Sure. Let's make up a haiku right now."

"Okay, but can you give me my baseball cards? I need inspiration."

Dad handed David the cards. David held them tightly and furrowed his brow. "Lis-ten, God, it's me," he counted five syllables on his fingers.

"Now seven syllables and then five again," Dad reminded him.

David closed his eyes to concentrate.

"Listen, God, it's me
Saying I'm very sorry
Hope you hear," David yawned, "my prayer."

"I think you're ready to be alone now," Dad patted David's head.

"I'm not alone. I can always talk to God," David whispered. "Good night, Dad."

Praised are You, God, who hears our prayers.

בָּרוּךְ אַתָּה שׁוֹמֵעַ תְּפִילָה.

Barukh atah shome'a tefilah.

4 ✡ Sukkot

Accepting Differences

Peace

Just a few days after Yom Kippur, on the 15th of Tishrei, Sukkot begins. It is a holiday of joy and thanksgiving that lasts seven days. The Kedners build a *sukkah*, a temporary hut to remind them of the huts the Israelites built when they wandered in the desert, and of the huts Israelite farmers built years later, when they came to Jerusalem to celebrate the harvest festival. Sukkot is the model for the American holiday of Thanksgiving.

David and Ilana love to eat in the *sukkah* all week. They also love the *lulav*—the palm branch with willow and myrtle branches—and the *etrog*, the citron. They wave the *lulav* and *etrog* in the synagogue, shaking them in all directions—east, south, west, north, up and down. That shows that all corners of the earth belong to God. At the end of Sukkot, the family celebrates *Shemini Atzeret*, during which there is a special prayer for rain so the crops in Israel can grow. All week long, Ilana and David greet friends and family with the words, *Hag Sameach*—Have a happy holiday!

Dad swept a pile of crinkly brown leaves into a corner of the yard. "We need a good spot for the sukkah," he muttered. He brushed away a yellow leaf that fell on the tip of his nose. "How did the Israelites build these huts while they wandered in the desert thousands of years ago? I bet they didn't worry about falling leaves, curious squirrels and..." he raised his voice, "...unhelpful children!"

Ilana and David stopped playing tag and skipped to Dad, jumping over the parts of the sukkah that were strewn on the grass. There were metal poles for the frame, a huge blue and yellow canvas to hang over the poles for walls, and long pine branches for the roof.

"Sorry, Dad," Ilana said breathlessly. "David was chasing me."

"You dared me!" David glared at her.

Dad ignored them. "Since we're building the sukkah on a Sunday when I'm off from work we have more time to do it properly," he said. "Remember last year...?"

"Don't remind us!" Ilana interrupted. "We built it at night and it leaned and swayed with every breeze as if it wanted to rub shoulders with the wind."

"Okay, so it was a sukkah you'll never forget, an indelible memory," Dad smiled. "Grab those poles and bring them to me." Ilana and David saluted and did as Dad asked. Dad joined the poles to make a rectangular frame.

"I could use more strong hands to help with the walls and roof," Dad said.

"We should have asked my friend Michelle," Ilana said. "She's only got one hand, but boy, is she strong. She tried to teach a bunch of us how to do one-handed cartwheels today. I can't even do cartwheels with two hands!"

"You and Michelle have really become buddies," Dad said. "Where's David? He seems to have disappeared. You and I had better talk and work at the same time or we may have a repeat of last year's Swaying Sukkah." He did a little Hawaiian dance, swaying his arms and his hips.

Ilana helped Dad drag the canvas to the frame. Dad climbed on a ladder and draped the canvas over the poles. "Instant walls!" he said. He wiped away a drop of sweat.

Ilana smoothed out the canvas. "You're right about Michelle," she said. "I used to be afraid to look at her because she was missing an arm. I was scared that might happen to me, until she explained she was born that way and it wasn't anybody's fault. She even joked about it. When some kindergartners asked what happened to her arm, she laughed and said a lion at the zoo ate it."

"How did you become friends?" Dad asked. "A pine branch, please."

Ilana hoisted a branch to Dad. "We worked on a science project together and found out that we both liked reading, we were both good in math, we both thought our younger brothers were pests, and we both loved ice cream."

"Did anybody ever tease Michelle?" Dad asked. He placed the branch across the top of the sukkah.

Ilana nodded and handed Dad another branch. "Once some boys made fun of her. She ignored them and walked away. But then I found her crying in the girls' bathroom. I told her I thought the boys were mean and that I was happy we were friends."

"You should feel proud for saying that, Ilana," Dad said, placing the second branch next to the first.

"It's not nice when people pick on other people just because they're different," Ilana said.

"Imagine if you and David were exactly the same, or if everyone in your class looked and behaved just like you," Dad agreed.

"Bor-ing!" Ilana rolled her eyes.

"Everyone is different, but we all use our own talents to make the world better," Dad said. He breathed in the woodsy fragrance. "I wish I could bottle this smell!" he said.

"We could name it *S'khakh* Scent!" Ilana clapped her hands. "The roof is called *s'khakh*," she explained to David, who had reappeared with a collection of sticks. "Say that fast five times!"

Dad climbed down the ladder, stepped back and surveyed the sukkah. "It's done!"

"Hooray," Ilana said. "It didn't fall down this year!"

Mom came out with boxes of decorations—Indian corn, strings of cranberries, apples and gourds, holiday cards, silk flowers and plastic fruit that looked real enough to eat. Ilana stood on the ladder and hung up whatever David handed to her. Soon the sukkah was wreathed in a hanging garden. Dad moved a table, four chairs and a little Oriental rug into the sukkah.

Ilana circled the sukkah slowly, taking in every detail. The card from Grandma and Grandpa with a drawing of children linking hands. The mobile she had made from red, green and yellow plastic apples that she had decorated with glitter and dangled from a hanger. The star of David her brother had fashioned from popsicle sticks. The Japanese lantern her mother hung in a special spot by the door. The gourds whose long crooked necks resembled the swans in the duck pond. The string of cranberries and green beans she had alternated in a mathematical pattern. The chain of baseball cards Dad had helped David to hang.

"It's more enchanting than the candy house Hansel and Gretel tried to eat," she said finally. "I wish we could invite the whole world to look up at the sun, the moon and the stars through the roof."

"It would be a little crowded in here!" Mom smiled.

"Can we at least invite Michelle and her father?" Ilana asked. Mom and Dad nodded.

"Wait a second," David cried. "Something's missing." He ran inside the house and returned with the lulav and etrog.

"This is *my* favorite part of Sukkot," he said. He shook the lulav, the tall

palm branch, so hard that it sounded like a chorus of maracas.

"Good thing I didn't put the myrtle and willow leaves on the lulav yet," Dad smiled. "They would have fallen right off." He took a straw holder shaped in a V, and put the myrtle into the right side and the willow into the left side. Then he attached the holder to the palm branch.

"I like the fact that each part of the lulav is different," Ilana said. "Just like people are different." She took the lulav and etrog from Dad. What a lemony scent the etrog had! Too bad its skin was so bumpy. The palm branch—the tall, stately spine of the lulav—didn't smell at all. She ran a finger carefully across the glossy myrtle leaves, blessed with both fragrance and beauty, then tried to straighten the droopy willows, which were neither beautiful nor fragrant.

"I think the parts of the lulav are like fractions," Ilana said. "When you add them all together, they make a perfect whole."

"A whole world," Dad said. "That's why we hold the lulav and etrog close together in our hands so they touch. When we wave them in six directions—north, east, south, west, up and down—it's like we're touching a whole world made up of people who are different."

"I'm glad there's a sukkah in my corner of the world," Ilana said. "Can we leave it up all the time so it could be a real home?"

"The sukkah isn't permanent. We only use it for a week," Dad answered.

"Thank you, God," David chimed out suddenly. "I love the sukkah!"

"Thank you, God," Dad echoed, "for giving us the strength to put up the sukkah without its falling down..."

"...for making each of us different and special like the lulav and etrog..." Ilana continued.

"...and for allowing us to live together with those differences in a *sukkat shalom*," Mom finished, "a sukkah of peace."

Praised are You, Adonai our God, who commanded us to take the lulav, to lift up the world and accept our differences.

בָּרוּךְ אַתָּה יְיָ, אֱלֹהֵינוּ מֶלֶךְ הָעוֹלָם, אֲשֶׁר קִדְּשָׁנוּ בְּמִצְוֹתָיו וְצִוָּנוּ עַל נְטִילַת לוּלָב.

Barukh atah Adonai, Elohenu melekh ha'olam, asher kideshanu bemitsvotav vetsivanu al netalat lulav.

5 ✡ Simchat Torah

It's Good to Be a Jew

Joyousness

Every Shabbat, Ilana, David and their parents listen to the Torah being read in the synagogue. It takes a year to complete reading the Torah. On Simchat Torah, which follows immediately after Sukkot, the Torah reading is completed and starts again from the very beginning. *Simchat Torah* means "joy in the Torah," and the Kedner family certainly does rejoice, by singing and dancing as all the Torahs are carried around the synagogue in seven special miniparades called *hakafot*. The children wave flags and enjoy a snack of apples and chocolate at the end of the service. Every adult has a chance to have an *aliyah*, to be called to the Torah and recite a blessing before and after it is read. Before the final reading, David, Ilana and all the children receive a special *aliyah* together.

David wondered whether he was in the synagogue or in Yankee Stadium on opening day. People who usually shushed him on Shabbat morning were stamping their feet and clapping. Rabbi Aaron and Dad were wearing baseball caps backwards. The cantor, who led the prayers, had donned a cowboy hat and was singing Hebrew words to the melody of *Take Me Out to the Ball Game!* Children were waving colorful paper flags.

"Is it too loud for you here?" Mom asked him. "On Simchat Torah grownups and children are supposed to be noisy and have fun. Almost anything goes."

Rabbi Aaron leaned forward into the microphone. "*Hag Sameach* everyone!" he said. "Happy Simchat Torah. Tonight we're going to sing and dance and celebrate being Jewish—things we don't do often enough. Simchat Torah is the perfect time to show our joy. So... let the dancing begin!"

All the Torahs in the ark were taken out. People took turns carrying them up and down the aisles and in the open space at the back of the synagogue. Ilana and her friends made a circle and danced the hora around the Torahs.

"David," Ilana called out. "We need you."

David looked around. People were bunched together in little groups, talking. Besides Ilana's friends, few others were dancing. "No way," he hung back.

"Come outside with me, David," Mom said, taking his hand.

David sat down cross-legged in the hallway. "You're not going to force me to dance, are you?" He folded his arms.

"People are a little nervous about dancing in synagogue," Mom said. "I remember the first time I came to a Simchat Torah celebration I didn't want to dance either. I thought the synagogue was just for praying and studying."

"How did you change your mind?" David asked.

"I realized that singing and dancing are ways of expressing our deepest feelings about being Jewish. They show that nothing can get us down."

"When you're sad sometimes I sing 'Skidamarink adink adoo I love you,' and you cheer up right away," David said.

"That's right," Mom said. "Music helps us overcome sadness. Singing and dancing and celebrating have helped keep Judaism alive."

"Judaism can die?" David asked, wide-eyed.

"What's your favorite flower in our garden?" Mom asked.

"Definitely the daffodils at springtime. Now that it's fall I like pumpkins and those flowers that are named for you."

"You mean chrysanthemums?" Mom laughed and tousled David's hair. "Suppose we didn't water them and care for them. Suppose the sun didn't shine on them. What would happen to them?"

"They would die," David replied.

"Judaism is like those flowers," Mom said. "If we don't care for it and water it with our joy, it can also die."

"But the flowers die after a while anyway," David said.

"That's where Judaism is different from a plant. If we care for it by studying, praying, singing and dancing, it will always live." Mom listened to the singing. "They're playing your song, David," she said.

David sang along. "*David, melekh yisra'el, chai, chai vekayam.*" He loved the song about David, the king of Israel who would live forever. Suddenly he stopped. "Look, Mom, Rabbi Aaron is dancing with Avi on his shoulders. Can I go on your shoulders?"

"Hop on!" Mom bent down and David climbed on. They joined the circle and began to dance. Other parents hoisted their children on their shoulders and the circle grew bigger. The people who carried the Torahs lifted the scrolls up in the air and the children leaned down to kiss the Torahs.

"I want to carry a Torah," Mom said. David clambered off. She chose a Torah with a green velvet cover and cradled it against her shoulder. "Do you want to help me carry it, David?"

David stared up at the Torah. At the Shabbat children's service he went to, he usually carried a very small Torah with a silky purple cover. He held it gently, like a baby. But this Torah was really big. "No thanks, Mom," he said.

"Just grasp one of the wooden holders at the bottom," Mom said softly. "We'll walk slowly."

David touched the holder. The wood felt smoother than his baseball bat against his fingertips. He stood on his tiptoes and stroked the soft, warm velvet cover.

Slowly, he started walking with Mom, pretending he was in a parade. A parade to God. He marched faster with a bounce in his step, still gripping the Torah tightly. All the children waved their paper flags. He saw Ilana and Dad dancing. Ilana caught his eye and winked. She pulled Dad and a line of friends into a circle around Mom and David.

"*David, melekh yisra'el,*" everybody sang, "*chai, chai vekayam!*"

David felt as proud as a king.

May we rejoice and be glad in celebrating a new year of Torah and in renewing our lives as Jews.

שִׂישׂוּ וְשִׂמְחוּ בְּשִׂמְחַת תּוֹרָה.

Sisu vesimechu besimchat torah.

6 ✡ Hanukkah

Standing Up for Your Beliefs

Conviction

During the dark winter days, Ilana and David look forward to the bright lights of Hanukkah, which begins on the 25th day of the Hebrew month of Kislev. On each of the eight nights of Hanukkah, they light one more candle in the *hanukkiah*, a special menorah with holders for eight candles, plus one more for the *shamash* candle, which helps light all the others. They know the legend of the lights: When the Jews recaptured the Temple, cleaned it and rededicated it, they found only one jar of oil to light the menorah. But instead of lasting only one day, the oil burned brightly for eight days. *Hanukkah* means dedication.

Hanukkah foods fried in oil remind the family of the miracle of the oil. Potato pancakes, or latkes, are Grandma's favorite, but David loves to eat chocolate Hanukkah gelt shaped like golden coins and fluffy jelly donuts called *sufganiyot*. David and Ilana also like to play dreidel, a top with four Hebrew letters on it: *nun, gimmel, hay* and *shin*. The letters stand for the Hebrew words *Nes Gadol Hayah Sham*: A great miracle happened there. Ilana can't wait to get her presents, but even more, she can't wait to give her family and friends the gifts she's made herself.

Ilana emptied the box of Hanukkah candles, spilling out a waxy rainbow of colors. For the second night of Hanukkah, she needed to choose three candles: one for each night and one for the shamash candle that lit the other candles.

"I can't decide what the best colors would be," she sighed. "Not white. The weather took care of that." She looked out at the snowstorm swirling down in spirals of white. "Maybe yellow, for the gold wrapping on the chocolate Hanukkah gelt." She unwrapped a coin-shaped piece of chocolate and popped it into her mouth.

Dad rolled up the sleeves of his sweatshirt and flipped a latke that was sizzling in the frying pan. "How about brown, for latkes?" he suggested.

Ilana shook her head. "There aren't any brown candles in this box. Maybe orange, for the flames." She fingered the candles. "What's the color of bravery?" she asked. "Red? Blue?"

"Red. Definitely red," Mom said, waving a letter angrily in the air. "That's the color I'm seeing."

"I only see red on Mom's socks," said David, who was sitting on the floor, waiting for Ilana to play the dreidel game. He had lined up his dreidels next to a cup of pennies.

"Mom means she's angry," Dad explained. "She's sizzling like these latkes." He spooned applesauce into a ceramic bowl.

"The town is planning to tear down Pine Street Playground," Mom said. "They sold the land. It's going to become a gas station."

"I love that playground!" Ilana cried. "It has a tunnel you can crawl into. I used to take a flashlight inside and read. It was so cozy."

"I remember David's huge smile when he took his first ride on the swings there. He was just a toddler," Dad added.

"For the town, business is business," Mom said. "We're going to have to call a meeting of neighbors to organize a protest. It's hard to fight the town, but we have to try."

"The Maccabees fought people who were stronger than they were," David said. "Why can't we?"

"Good point, David," Dad smiled. "They stood up for what they thought was right."

"I know the story," Ilana said. "The Syrians captured the Temple in Jerusalem and filled it with idols. The Jews weren't allowed to pray, study or eat kosher food. Though the Maccabees were just a small group of Jews, they fought the Syrians, recaptured the Temple and cleaned it up."

She chose red, blue and orange candles and wiggled them firmly into the hanukkiah.

"We'll have to try for a modern-day Hanukkah miracle to save the playground," Dad said.

"Time to light the candles," Mom called. She turned off the lights. The family gathered around the antique brass menorah that had once belonged to Dad's great-grandparents. Mom had placed it on the windowsill so everyone outside could see it.

Dad lit the shamash candle first, then the other candles from left to right. Ilana held Dad's hand to light the first candle. The wick caught fire slowly, then leapt up brightly. David helped light the second candle.

"Barukh atah Adonai, Elohenu melekh ha'olam, asher kideshanu bemitsvotav

vetsivanu lehadlik ner shel hanukkah," they chanted together. "Praised are You, Adonai our God, who commanded us to light the Hanukkah lights."

After chanting another blessing thanking God for the miracle of Hanukkah, Mom began singing *Maoz Tzur.* Ilana and Dad joined in. Even David knew most of the words. "*Az egmor beshir mizmor, chanukat hamizbe'ach.*"

"I will sing a song of joy, recalling the rededication of the Temple," Mom sang, squishing the English translation into the melody.

When the song ended, everybody watched the candles silently. Like a mirror, the window reflected the flames. "I can see two sets of candles!" David whispered.

"Those dancing flames make me want to dance," Mom said. She put her arm around Dad's waist and swept him into a waltz, humming the tune of *Hanukkah, Oh Hanukkah!*

"No more temper?" Dad teased her. She shook her head. "But I haven't forgotten the playground," she said.

"Do we get presents tonight?" David asked.

"Remember we agreed on one gift the first night only," Mom said, still dancing. "Hanukkah is about the miracle of freedom, not the miracle of presents."

"But Mom," David argued, "All my friends get presents on other nights."

"We do have a little gift for you," Mom smiled, taking a small package wrapped in shiny paper out of a drawer.

David unwrapped it. "Finger puppets?" he squealed in disgust. "I was hoping for a train set."

"Dad and I thought it would be fun to hear the story of Hanukkah in your words," Mom said. "You could make a puppet show."

"You always have a game up your sleeve, Mom," Ilana said. "Oh well, David, let's try to make the best of it." She grabbed his hand and led him upstairs.

An hour later, they came back down. "You are invited to a puppet show," they bowed to Mom and Dad, who settled on the sofa. On a table, David set a carton from which he had cut out the back.

"Once there was a man named Judah M," Ilana began. Through the back of the carton, David waved a finger puppet with a big J on it. "Judah lived in a town called Presentville, where everyone spent all year planning their Hanukkah presents. But Judah had a tough job. Every day he went from house to house trying to convince the people of the town that there was more to Hanukkah than presents. First he visited Mrs. Latke." Ilana wiggled a puppet with a hat shaped like a potato pancake.

"Good morning, Mrs. Latke," David said in a deep voice. "Nice to see you so oily in the morning. Just wanted to remind you about the miracle of the Hanukkah oil, which burned in the Temple for eight days instead of just one. That's why we celebrate Hanukkah for eight days."

"My kids don't care about the Hanukkah story," Ilana said in Mrs. Latke's grouchy voice. "They just want their presents."

"Judah visited the dreidel twins next," David said. "But like Mrs. Latke, they insisted they only had time for presents." Ilana spun two puppets shaped like tops.

"Judah went to Mr. Gelt's store and Miss Candle's school. Nobody was interested in the Hanukkah story," Ilana continued. "Then one day, the king of Presentville ordered that the townspeople could no longer fry latkes, spin dreidels or light Hanukkah candles. And they could only give one present. Everyone gathered in Menorah Square. They wondered what to do."

"We have to stand up for what we believe in," David said in Judah's voice. "Now's the time to show what Hanukkah really means."

"Presents are okay, but I want to remember the miracle of the oil," Ilana said in Mrs. Latke's voice.

"The townspeople sent letters of protest," David said. "When the king realized that the people finally understood the meaning of Hanukkah, he allowed them to celebrate the holiday. The end."

Mom and Dad clapped. "You've put your fingers right on the meaning of Hanukkah," Dad said. "Bravo!"

"The candles have gone out already," Mom said, "but your play shows that the Hanukkah story keeps burning strong in all kinds of ways. And now, I'm sure the stars of the show are hungry. Latkes, everyone!"

**Praised are You,
Adonai our God,
who has inspired us
to stand up for our beliefs.**

בָּרוּךְ אַתָּה יְיָ, אֱלֹהֵינוּ מֶלֶךְ הָעוֹלָם,
שֶׁעָשָׂה נִסִּים לַאֲבוֹתֵינוּ בַּיָּמִים
הָהֵם בַּזְּמַן הַזֶּה.

Barukh atah Adonai, Elohenu melekh
ha'olam, she'asah nisim la'avotenu
bayamim hahem bazeman hazeh.

7 ✡ Tu B'Shevat
Caring for Nature
Wonder

David and Ilana often wonder how old the trees in their backyard are. While they don't know exactly when the trees were planted, they like to celebrate the trees' "birthday" on Tu B'Shevat, the Jewish new year for trees. Tu B'Shevat is like a Jewish Arbor Day; it falls on the 15th day of the Hebrew month of Shevat. While Tu B'Shevat is a winter holiday in America, in the land of Israel it's a time when the first buds appear on trees.

The Kedners plant trees on Tu B'Shevat and celebrate with a special *seder*, a ceremony celebrating the fruits of Israel, adapted from the Pesach *seder* (ritual meal). They drink four cups of wine or grape juice—dark red, light red, pink and white—to represent the changes in the seasons. They eat fruits and nuts mentioned in the Bible, like dates and figs. They also try to eat different kinds of fruit: those with coverings on the outside, like oranges; those with pits, like peaches and olives; and those that can be eaten inside and outside, like raisins. While it is still winter, Ilana and David love to think about the earth blooming again.

"Look up at that maple tree, David," Grandpa said. "There are five woodpecker holes."

"Did the woodpecker make them like this, Grandpa?" David hugged the tree and bobbed his head back and forth.

Grandpa laughed. "You need a sharper nose, kiddo."

"Mom says I have a sharp nose," David sniffed. "She says I can smell chocolate chip cookies in my sleep." He walked around the tree. "There's a big hole here. I'm going to climb in."

"First you're a woodpecker. Now you're a squirrel! I thought it was David who was walking in the woods with me," Grandpa teased.

"It is!" David popped out from behind the tree and his list for the Tu B'Shevat seder fell out of his pocket. "I want to collect some things to decorate the seder table on Tu B'Shevat," he said, pouncing on it.

"In my day we just sent money to plant trees in Israel," Grandpa said.

"We still do that," David said. "But the seder is cool. We don't have to wait as long to eat as we do on Pesach. There are fruits and nuts that grow here and in Israel, like dates, figs, grapes and almonds, and yummy wheat crackers. It's a party for nature."

"I'm glad you're learning to enjoy things that grow from the earth," Grandpa said. "It's easy to forget that apples and bananas don't appear magically on our plates."

"I know," David said. "First someone has to plant the seeds, water them and pluck the weeds. Then someone has to watch the food grow and pick it just when it's ready." He spied a pine cone. "This would be a great decoration. Let's collect more."

The trees glistened. David touched icicles hanging from bare branches.

"Wow, Grandpa," he said, "I can see rainbows when the sun shines on the icicles."

A little further, Grandpa pointed out a pine tree. "I wonder why these needles are green and everything around them is brown," David said.

"I used to wonder how a bare tree blossoms again each spring," Grandpa said.

"My turn," David said. "I wonder how the sky turns pink and purple and orange and yellow when the sun sets."

"Hmmm," Grandpa stroked his chin. "I wonder how you got to be smart enough to ask such good questions!"

"Thanks, Grandpa," David smiled. "Seriously, I wonder about thunder and lightning. It's spooky in the dark when it thunders."

"Sometimes the world can be scary," Grandpa said. "There are earthquakes and floods and tornadoes. But a tornado can also be amazing. How does it move so fast? Earthquakes and floods are amazing. How does the earth split? Why do the waves swell so high?"

"Maybe I'll learn the answers in school," David said.

"We can't do anything to stop earthquakes, floods and tornadoes," Grandpa said, "but we can still do a lot to be part of nature."

"Do we have to become farmers?" David asked. "I'd like to ride on a tractor."

"It's hard to believe," Grandpa said, "but just looking around us is the first step. We can watch for crocuses when they poke up from the ground in the spring. We can play in the leaves when they turn gold and red and brown in the fall. During the summer, we can listen to birds sing. Even now, when it seems like nothing is alive, we can watch squirrels scampering up the trees."

"I just saw one," David nodded. "He's probably looking for acorns. I'm hungry too." He took an apple out of his pocket. "I'll save the seeds to plant," he said. "Remember last year when we planted marigold seeds on Tu B'Shevat? I love to squish my hands in the dirt."

David picked up rocks of different shapes, bird feathers, pieces of fallen bark, acorns and more pine cones. "I found a candy wrapper, Grandpa," he said.

Grandpa frowned. "Put it in your pocket until we get home. If we want the world to be beautiful, we can't just admire it, we have to take care of it. There's no abracadabra."

"What if we don't take care of it?" David asked.

"Imagine a world without trees and grass," Grandpa said, "without sand and sun, clean air and water."

"It would feel as if the earth were under a deep dark spell," David said. He picked up two maple seedlings. "But these look like magical angels' wings."

"What's really magical is that from those tiny seeds sprout huge maples," Grandpa said.

David looked up. The sky was blue. "If nature is magical," he said, "I want it to snow. Abracadabra, let it snow. Bibbidi bobbidi boo. Right now." He waved his arms like a magician. His fingers fluttered like snowflakes.

Grandpa laughed. "Magicians *are* amazing, David. But even they can't make the snow fall or tell the rain to stop. That's why nature fills us with wonder. The world is alive with magic, from the smallest seedlings in your hand to the tallest trees in the woods."

"Hey, Grandpa, guess what kind of Tu B'Shevat celebration we're having right now?" David grinned. "A magic show!"

Praised are You, Adonai our God, who has allowed us to live to this day to say Wow! about the world.

בָּרוּךְ אַתָּה יְיָ, אֱלֹהֵינוּ מֶלֶךְ הָעוֹלָם,
שֶׁהֶחֱיָנוּ וְקִיְּמָנוּ וְהִגִּיעָנוּ לַזְּמַן הַזֶּה.

Barukh atah Adonai, Elohenu melekh ha'olam,
shehecheyanu vekiyemanu
vehigi'anu lazman hazeh.

8 ✡ Purim
Giving Instead of Taking
Gratitude

In their Purim play, Mom, Dad, Ilana and David explain that Purim commemorates the occasion on which Esther and Mordecai saved the Jewish people. The villainous Haman chose the 13th of Adar to destroy the Jews of Persia. When his plot was foiled, the following day became one of celebration, Purim.

The Kedners bake *hamentaschen*, shaped like the three-cornered hat Haman is said to have worn. They include *hamentaschen* in their *mishloach manot*, baskets of food they deliver to neighbors, relatives and friends. They greet everyone with the expression *Simchat Purim*—Happy Purim.

On Purim the Kedners go to synagogue to read *Megillat Esther*, the Scroll of Esther, which recounts the story of Purim. Each time Ilana and David hear Haman's name, they drown it out with noisemakers called *groggers*. Ilana and David enjoy the Purim carnival at the synagogue. Friends invite them to a traditional Purim *se'udah*, a fun-filled meal with humorous skits or stories. Mrs. Friedman, their neighbor, follows the Purim tradition of *matanot l'ev-yonim*, giving gifts of food, clothing or money to poor people. By visiting her, the Kedners fulfill the Jewish obligation of *bikur cholim*, visiting the sick, a responsibility they take seriously all year.

David sat on a stool and kicked his legs against the kitchen counter. Thump-a-rump. Thump-a-rump. He was eyeing a gooey ball of dough that was ready to be rolled into hamentaschen.

"A tiny taste wouldn't hurt, would it?" he asked Ilana.

"Go for it," she grinned, "before Mom and Dad come back."

As he reached to break off a piece, Mom and Dad returned. "Aha!" Mom said. "We saw that!"

"Mrs. Friedman always lets us taste the dough when we bake chocolate chip cookies with her," David said. "It's the best part."

"Mrs. Friedman is my favorite neighbor," Ilana added. "She always has a new library book for me to read."

"I'm worried about her," Mom said, rolling out the dough. "She was in an accident. The doctor said she has to stay home for a week. She'll miss celebrating Purim in the synagogue."

"Let's take Purim to her," Ilana said, using a glass to cut the dough into circles. "We can bring her a basket of hamentaschen and act out the Purim story."

"Hats off to you for that idea," Dad said, spooning prune, poppyseed and apricot fillings onto the dough.

David wrinkled his nose. "You'll spoil this yummy dough with that prune and poppyseed stuff Grandma and Grandpa like."

"Let's make cherry and chocolate chip hamentaschen instead!" Ilana declared.

"Who says we can't have something new and exciting?" Dad agreed.

Ilana and David filled circles of dough with cherries and chocolate chips. Mom and Dad shaped them into triangles. Even Frisky the dog got some flour on his nose and gobbled the chips that fell under the table. While the hamentaschen were baking, Ilana and David made get-well cards for Mrs. Friedman. Later, they filled a basket with apples, oranges, bananas, Tootsie Rolls, peanuts, almonds and the cooled hamentaschen.

"Time for costumes for the Purim play! I'm Mordecai the hero!" David sang out. He put on a blue bathrobe and a long beard of cotton balls from the dress-up box. Ilana chose a blue silk dress embroidered with gold. "I'm Esther the heroine," she called.

"I'll be King Ahasuerus," Dad said. Ilana brought him a crown.

Mom drew a pointy black beard on her chin with face paints. "I'll be the bad guy—wicked Haman," she said with a nasty chuckle. "Ha ha ha."

"Oooh, Mom, you're scary," Ilana pretended to shiver.

Everyone walked together to Mrs. Friedman's house. Her daughter Joni answered the door and welcomed them inside.

"We're sorry you're not feeling well," Ilana said, hugging Mrs. Friedman. She was sitting on the sofa with her leg in a cast.

"Happy Purim," David said. He gave her the basket and a hug.

"Hamentaschen! These look as delicious as the hugs you just gave me," Mrs. Friedman smiled.

"We brought the story of Purim to you," Ilana said. "Except we need a narrator and Queen Vashti."

"I'll be Vashti," Joni said. "I have the perfect red silk kimono to wear."

"I do a terrific narrator," Mrs. Friedman said. "Joni, could you get my rainbow-colored wig?"

When Mrs. Friedman and Joni were in costume, Mrs. Friedman began the story. "Once upon a time, in the city of Shushan, Persia, there lived a king named Ahasuerus who liked to party."

"That's me," said Dad. "I invited my queen, Vashti, to one of my feasts, but can you believe it, she said, 'No way.'" Joni swished her kimono from side to side and shook her head defiantly.

"The king didn't like her attitude, so he kicked her out of the kingdom," Mrs. Friedman continued. "He held a beauty contest and chose Esther to be his new queen." Ilana twirled around. "But Esther was more than just a pretty face. She was wise enough to listen carefully to her Uncle Mordecai."

David jumped out. "Remember Esther, my dear niece," he wagged his finger at Ilana, "you may be queen, but you can't tell anyone who you are. Nobody in the palace can know you're Jewish."

"Nobody?" Ilana asked. "Not even the king? Uncle Mordecai, that would be like nobody knowing my name!"

"It's not easy being Jewish in Persia," David answered. "Who knows what the king would do if he found out?"

Mrs. Friedman went on. "King Ahasuerus had a wicked adviser named Haman. Everybody in the kingdom bowed down to him. But Mordecai refused. He would only bow down to God. Haman got so angry that he convinced the king to kill all the Jews."

Mom rubbed her hands together gleefully. "Who needs people who are different from us!" she snarled.

"You are the only one who can stop Haman, Esther dear," David said to Ilana. "It's all up to you. But don't worry. I have a plan." He whispered in Ilana's ear. "Psst, psst, psst..."

"Esther invited Ahasuerus and Haman to two parties," Mrs. Friedman said. "This is what happened at the second party."

"Nice party, Esther," Dad said. "I'll grant you any wish."

"Haman wants to kill all the Jews," Ilana said. "I am Jewish, too. You must save my people from that wicked man!" She pointed to Mom. Mom clutched her throat and gasped. "Hang him!" Dad shouted.

"So they did," Mrs. Friedman concluded. "Esther gave away some of her goodness and bravery, and in return, she saved the Jews of Persia. To celebrate, the Jews of Shushan gave *mishloach manot*—gifts to each other.

They also gave *matanot l'evyonim*, gifts to poor people."

"That's still how we celebrate Purim today!" David announced. "The end."

Everyone bowed. "Children," Mrs. Friedman clapped loudly, "You've given me the best *mishloach manot* ever. And don't think I've forgotten about you." She nodded to Joni, who pulled out two baskets from behind the sofa. They were filled with books and bags of chocolate chip cookies.

**There was light, joy,
gladness and honor
for the Jewish people.**

לַיְּהוּדִים הָיְתָה אוֹרָה וְשִׂמְחָה
וְשָׂשׂוֹן וִיקָר.

Layehudim hayetah orah vesimchah
vesason vikar.

9 ✡ Pesach
"I Was at Sinai"
Continuity

Passover (*Pesach* in Hebrew) is the springtime holiday celebrating the Exodus from Egypt. While Pesach starts on the 15th of Nisan, the Kedners begin their preparations a few weeks before. They clean their home thoroughly to remove all their *chametz*, leavened food. During the week of Pesach, *chametz* symbolizes the luxuries the Jews could not enjoy as they prepared to leave Egypt. On the night before Pesach, Ilana, David and their parents search the house for *chametz* while holding a candle, a wooden spoon and a feather. They burn the *chametz* the next morning.

Ilana and David help fill the *seder* plate with the traditional foods that represent different parts of the Exodus story. The Kedners invite family, friends, and guests to their *seder* (a ritual meal). They read from a *haggadah* (Hebrew for "telling") which features the story of the Exodus, songs, rituals and interpretations about the meaning of freedom. Ilana and Grandma explore creative ways to experience the *seder*; they include other examples of freedom and slavery.

Ilana stretched a sheet over the sofa in the family room. She knotted the ends together with another sheet, draped the second sheet over a chair, and surveyed her work.

"Looks pretty good, Ilana," Grandma nodded.

"We wanted something fun for the kids to do at the seder," Ilana said. "We decided to make a tent so we could feel like we actually left Egypt. Remember last year we did a play on the ten plagues? David dressed up as a frog and I was a disgusting locust. All our cousins came dressed as different plagues."

"In my day," Grandma sighed, "we recited every single word of the haggadah but we didn't stop to explain."

"Weren't you bored?" Ilana asked.

"Except when we looked for the *afikoman*, we had to sit still," Grandma replied. "I liked to sing *Dayenu* and *Ma Nishtanah*, but I didn't really understand most of the chanting or the grownups' conversation."

"Was there anything fun about your seder?"

Grandma chuckled. "Every ten minutes my Aunt Helen would wink at Uncle Herman, who was conducting the seder. It was her way of asking him when she should serve the meal. All the kids winked at him too. We were starving."

"That is funny, Grandma," Ilana grinned. "But our seder is more fun now. Look at this tent, though. You think it's good? I think it's a disaster."

"We need something higher to anchor it," Grandma said. "What if we take down those hanging plants and use the hooks in the ceiling?"

"Grandma, you're a genius!" Ilana jumped up.

"Maybe, but I'm not as young as I used to be," Grandma laughed. "How are we going to reach those hooks?"

"I'll be right back." Ilana ran out of the room and returned with a stepladder from the garage. She climbed up, handed the plants to Grandma and hung the sheets between the hooks. "Welcome to night-time in Egypt," she intoned.

"I can feel the sand between my toes," Grandma said.

"Don't get too comfy," Ilana said. "Tonight we're leaving Egypt."

"Oh my!" Grandma exclaimed. "There's so much to get ready and so little time! What should we take with us?"

"My toothbrush," Ilana joked.

"I don't think they knew about fluoride back then," Grandma joked back.

"Okay, I'll take my favorite doll, Miriam. I named her after Moses's sister."

"Wear something comfortable," Grandma warned. "After the meal tonight, we're leaving immediately. Now what will we eat on the way?"

"Mom already baked something called matzah. She was hoping to bake bread but Moses told us to be quick. The yeast didn't have time to rise. The matzah is as flat as a piece of papyrus."

"I feel terrible that I won't have time to bake my famous Egyptian date muffins," Grandma said with a twinkle in her eye. "I'll take my kneading trough anyway. Maybe I can open a bakery in the Promised Land, where we're going. I've already thought of a name—Promised Land Pastries."

"We'll be thirsty," Ilana added. "I'll go to the well and fill a jug with water."

"This is really working, Ilana," Grandma said. "I feel like we're actually back in Egypt. Will we chant the whole haggadah in the tent?"

"We'll start here to set the mood," Ilana answered. "Maybe we should ask

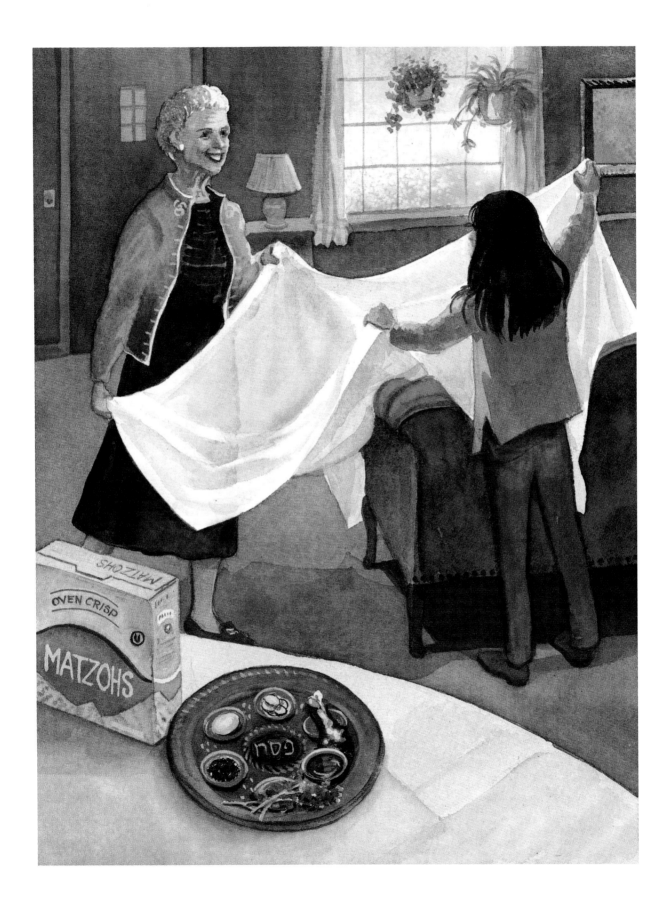

each guest to bring a backpack filled with things they would take if they were leaving Egypt."

"During the part of the haggadah when the Israelites actually leave, we can walk around the house with our backpacks," Grandma said.

"Cool," Ilana nodded.

Suddenly Grandma was silent. "This is not just an old story," she said finally, wiping a tear from her eye. "I remember packing in a hurry when I had to leave my home in Germany. Had we not left, our enemies, the Nazis, would have killed us all."

"What did you take with you, Grandma?"

"All I had time to pack were a few clothes," Grandma said. "We were just lucky to get out alive."

"I can't picture not having my dolls, my toys and my books," Ilana sighed. "You must have been so scared."

"Just like the Israelites must have been during the night of the exodus from Egypt," Grandma answered.

"I read a book about another exodus from a country called Ethiopia," Ilana said. "The Jews had to leave their homes because their lives were in danger. They traveled thousands of miles by foot to reach airplanes which took them to Israel."

"I have another story. You know cousin Gideon who lives in Jerusalem?" Grandma asked. "His father fought in the Yom Kippur War in 1973 to defend Israel's borders. Part of the war was fought in Egypt. The Israeli soldiers were lucky to leave Egypt alive."

"Wow!" Ilana exclaimed. "Pesach is not just a story in a tent. I can't believe how many real kinds of exodus there have been."

"You and your friends take your freedom for granted sometimes," Grandma said.

"My friends and I are lucky. We've never been in danger because we're Jewish," Ilana agreed. "It's because of people who were brave enough to escape danger—like you, Grandma—that we can still celebrate being free the way the Israelites did at Sinai."

In every generation we should picture ourselves leaving Egypt and standing at Sinai.

בְּכָל־דּוֹר וָדוֹר חַיָּב אָדָם לִרְאוֹת אֶת עַצְמוֹ כְּאִלּוּ הוּא יָצָא מִמִּצְרָיִם.

Bekhol-dor vador chayav adam lirot et atsmo ke'ilu hu yatsa mimitsrayim.

10 ✡ Yom Ha-shoah

Why Doesn't God Stop the Bad Guys?
Free Will

Soon after Israel became a country, the new Israeli government created Yom Ha-shoah, the 27th of Nisan, to memorialize the six million Jews and five million other people the Nazis killed. The Kedner family—especially Ilana's grandmother, a Holocaust survivor—participates in a Yom Ha-shoah service. Ilana and her friends begin the service by carrying in memorial candles. Her grandmother and other survivors talk about their experiences and read prayers, poems, and personal accounts of what happened during the Holocaust. The service is one of both sadness and hope for the future, and usually includes the *El Maleh Rachamim* memorial prayer and the *Mourner's Kaddish*. Ilana and her grandmother hope that both young and elderly will dedicate themselves to renewing Jewish life, while never forgetting the Holocaust.

Mom hit the power button on the television and shut it off. "I feel like kicking this TV," she muttered. "There's too much bad news."

"The announcer spoke about mean kids who threw rocks at swans in the park," Ilana said. "Then he talked about people who died when a bomb exploded."

Mom whirled around. "I didn't notice you sitting there," she said. "I thought you were doing your homework."

"I was," Ilana said. "We came down for a snack. Mom, will those people be punished?"

"I'm sure the police are doing whatever they can," Mom said.

Ilana stared at her sandwich. She was scared. Maybe those people would set a bomb in her neighborhood. She looked up at the framed picture of Grandma that hung on the wall. It was taken in Germany when Grandma was nine years old. Even though the picture was black and white, Grandma had told her the dress was sky-blue. Matching blue ribbons were looped through her braids.

Ilana shuddered. Grandma had also told her that just a few days after that picture was taken, the Nazis had looted and destroyed all the Jewish stores in her neighborhood. They had smashed every window in waves of crashing glass that splintered in the street. She and her brothers had heard everything. They were hiding in the attic of their house.

Mom looked at Ilana, who was still staring at Grandma's picture. "Is Grandma's story worrying you?" Mom asked softly. She put her arm around Ilana. "It's okay to be scared, Ilana. Bad things are frightening."

"Are you talking about bad guys?" David asked. "I'm going to help catch them. Pow. Pow." He pretended his fingers were guns.

"Catching bad guys isn't a game, David," Mom said. "The good guys don't always win like they do in storybooks and fairy tales."

"I know it's Yom Ha-shoah tonight, when we remember the Holocaust. Grandma was telling me about it," Ilana said in a small voice. "The good guys sure didn't win in the city where she grew up. Grandma was one of the few lucky ones the Nazis didn't kill."

"Who are the Nazis?" David asked.

"When Grandma was a child in Germany, there were people called Nazis who wanted to be powerful," Mom said. "They followed a leader named Adolf Hitler. He told them that to be powerful, they had to kill anyone who was different from them. Hitler said Jewish people were so different that they should all be destroyed. The Nazis killed six million Jews and five million other innocent people."

"Millions?" David asked. "It would take me forever to count that high. How could anyone kill that many people?"

"How are Jewish people different, anyway?" Ilana asked. "We look the same as other people. We breathe. We eat. We sleep. We have faces and bodies and hands and feet."

"Yeah, we're not monsters!" David added.

"It's almost impossible to believe so many were killed," Mom said. "Not even grownups really understand. But people in other countries let Hitler take over their governments and helped him to do the terrible things he planned."

She turned to Ilana. "Your question is hard to answer also. Jewish people have been small in number wherever we've lived. We've observed different holidays and customs. Even though it's unfair and cruel, it was easy for people like the Nazis to blame the Jewish people for their problems." She paused. "It's time to leave for the ceremony now."

The lights were dimmed in the hallway of the synagogue. People talked quietly to one another. Ilana clutched a thick yellow candle in a glass, a memorial candle that reminded people not to forget those who had died. Ten other children were lined up at the doorway to the sanctuary, holding candles. Next to each child stood an older man or woman who had survived the Holocaust.

"One candle for each million," Ilana heard Grandma say. Grandma came up behind Ilana and kissed her.

"I'm nervous, Grandma," Ilana said. Grandma squeezed her hand gently as the piano began to play. "Time to march in," Grandma whispered.

Ilana took a deep breath and walked into the sanctuary. It was so quiet she could hear Grandma breathe next to her. Someone had turned off the lights. Only the eleven candles flickering slowly forward lit up the darkness. The children carried them to a table in the front of the sanctuary. Then the lights came on.

"Thanks for walking with me, bubbaleh," Grandma whispered. She went to sit with Grandpa.

When the service ended and most of the people had left, Mom and Ilana remained in their seats at the back of the synagogue. Ilana leaned against Mom's shoulder.

"I can't stop wondering if anybody tried to fight back against the Nazis," she said.

"At first, nobody could believe the Nazis were going to kill them," Mom answered. "By the time they realized what was happening, they usually couldn't escape. The Nazis put the Jews into small areas called ghettos where they watched their every move. Then they put them into concentration camps. Many died there. But some very brave people tried to fight back—even children."

"Why do people do such bad things?" Ilana asked.

"We don't always know," Mom shook her head. "Sometimes they don't learn the difference between good and bad. They may only think of what's good for themselves, no matter how it hurts others. They may want to get back at people who don't do what they say. That makes them feel powerful."

"Can't anyone stop them?" Ilana asked. "Can't God stop them? God is more powerful than they are. How could God allow bad things to happen?"

"God gave us the rules that teach us what's right and wrong," Mom answered. "God hopes we will choose to be kind, fair, loving and good. That would make God happy."

Ilana shut her eyes. She could still see the candles flickering like golden birds in cages. "Maybe God should decide that all people should choose good," she said. "Then there wouldn't be evil in the world."

"Just imagine if Dad and I never allowed you to make choices," Mom said. "You couldn't choose whether to wear your red shirt or your blue one. You couldn't choose whether to eat macaroni and cheese or peanut butter and jelly. You couldn't choose what to read at bedtime."

"I'd feel like a prisoner!" Ilana said, opening her eyes.

"That's why it's also up to us to choose between good and bad," Mom continued. "Even if it hurts God when we don't make the right choice, it's still up to us."

"But the Holocaust wasn't just a wrong choice like sneaking a candy bar before dinner," Ilana said. "When Grandma told me how much the Nazis hurt her and her family, I wanted to cry."

"As horrible as the Holocaust was," Mom said, stroking Ilana's hair, "God didn't stop it. God was sad to see the hatred and destruction, but once God gave us the freedom to choose, the world was left to us. That's a big responsibility."

"What can we do?" Ilana asked. "We're just kids."

"More than you think," Mom said. "You already know what can happen when people hate each other. That's the first step. When one person hates, that hatred touches a second person, then a third person, and a fourth and a fifth, until it spreads to lots of people. When the Nazis hated, their hatred spread until millions of Jews died—parents, grand-parents, children, brothers, sisters, aunts, uncles, cousins, friends."

"I wish people could be kind instead of hateful," Ilana said. "The world would be a lot less scary." She shut her eyes again and tried to picture the world that way. She saw the golden birds flying free.

Praised are You, Adonai our God, who has made me free to choose between right and wrong.

בָּרוּךְ אַתָּה יְיָ, אֱלֹהֵינוּ מֶלֶךְ הָעוֹלָם,
שֶׁעָשַׂנִי בֶּן\בַּת חוֹרִין.

Barukh atah Adonai, Elohenu melekh ha'olam,
she'asani ben/bat chorin.

11 ✡ Yom Ha-atzma'ut
We Care About One Another
Community

Ilana and David have a special place in their hearts for Israel. In school and at home, they learn about Israel's land, history, people and holy sites. They learn how Jews who once lived in dangerous places now live safely in Israel. Ilana and David celebrate Yom Ha-atzma'ut on the fifth of Iyar—the Hebrew date in 1948 when Israel became a country. They learn Israeli songs and dances, eat Israeli foods such as falafel, hummus and pita, and write to their Israeli pen-pals.

While Mom and Dad enjoy watching Ilana march in the annual Israel parade, they also read newspapers, magazines and articles about the peace process in Israel. They are planning a trip to Israel for Ilana's Bat Mitzvah, and hope to visit often in the future.

Yom Ha-atzma'ut celebrations might also include special prayers and a Torah and Haftarah reading in the synagogue morning service, or a fair with Israeli products, clothes, books and entertainment.

Ilana sat knee to knee with Aunt Sharon on the sofabed in the guest room. A big photo album was open between them. "You look like a mummy bobbing in water in this picture," Ilana laughed. "A mummy in a bathing suit." She took the photo out of its plastic sleeve and squinted at it. "How did you float like that?"

"The water in the Dead Sea is so salty that you float without even trying," replied Aunt Sharon, who was visiting for a few days. Ilana loved her like a big sister. "It's one of the most fun places in Israel."

Ilana pointed to another picture, of a woman in a long black-and-yellow dress sitting under a palm tree. "Who's this?"

"An immigrant who just arrived in Israel from Yemen," Aunt Sharon replied.

"Look at those beads she's wearing around her neck!" Ilana exclaimed. "What a spiderweb of colors!"

"Jewelry is a special Yemenite craft," Aunt Sharon said. "Once, many

Jews lived in Yemen, a country in the Middle East. Soon after Israel became a country in 1948, the Israeli government decided to bring most of the Yemenite Jews to Israel. Yemen wasn't safe for Jews anymore. The secret mission was called Operation Magic Carpet."

"Are you talking about Aladdin's magic carpet?" David asked. He whizzed around the room, holding his arms out airplane-style.

"No, this is a true story," Aunt Sharon said. "But you're on the right track. The magic carpet was a plane. Most of the Yemenite Jews lived in such simple conditions that they had never even heard of a plane. They thought a big bird was taking them to Israel."

"Big Bird?" David joked. "First you talk about Aladdin and now Sesame Street? What's going on here?"

Aunt Sharon laughed. "This story is not make-believe. It's real-life magic. Not all the Jews left Yemen the first time, so a few years ago, Israel planned another secret mission and rescued most of the rest."

"Why does Israel care about what happens to Jews in another country?" Ilana asked.

"Jews have always taken care of other Jews. No matter where we live, we think of ourselves as one people. We care for one another as if we were part of one big community." Aunt Sharon paused. "Name any country in the world."

"India," Ilana said.

"There are Jews from India in Israel. Name another."

"Russia," David said.

Aunt Sharon nodded. "There are Jews from Russia in Israel. There are Jews from Morocco and Turkey and Canada; there are Jews from Brazil and Argentina, from England and America."

"Is there room for so many Jews?" David asked. "I thought Israel was a small country."

"Israel welcomes all Jews, even if the government has to build houses in the desert or on mountaintops," Aunt Sharon answered.

"In the desert? Such a hot, bare place?" David asked.

"The hot desert was better than the dangerous places Jews lived before," Aunt Sharon explained. "Some loved Israel so much they didn't care where they lived. Others were determined to make the desert blossom."

"Flowers and vegetables growing out of the sand?" Ilana shook her head in amazement.

Aunt Sharon nodded. "I was in Israel on Yom Ha-atzma'ut—Israel Independence Day," she said. "The streets were filled with people singing and dancing, celebrating together as Jews in one big birthday party. It didn't matter where we came from. I felt as if the whole country was my family."

"Do they have barbecues and fireworks like we have on the Fourth of July?" David asked.

"That's an American custom," Aunt Sharon answered. "But oh, what food they have! I tasted a kind of bread called melawah, from Yemen; tandoori chicken from India; a stew called goulash from Hungary, and good old Israeli falafel. For dessert, there were spicy cardamom cookies from Iran, chocolate babka from Russia and jelly donuts from America. But everything had a special Israeli taste. What did you do here to celebrate Yom Ha-atzma'ut?"

"In Hebrew school we had cupcakes decorated with blue-and-white icing and tiny Israeli flags," David said.

"My class marched in a parade for Israel," Ilana added. "It sounds like the celebration in Israel. We sang and danced. Crowds of people stood on the sidewalk and cheered. For our float, we built a model of the city of Ashkelon, our sister city in Israel. Our class had a pen-pal project with a school in Ashkelon."

"What's your pen-pal's name?" Aunt Sharon asked.

"Yael," Ilana said. "She's 11. Our class collected money to help build a new playground in Ashkelon. Our friends in Ashkelon sent us ten dozen Israeli oranges. They were so juicy I needed three napkins to eat one orange!"

"Will you ever meet Yael?" David asked.

"She invited me to visit her," Ilana answered. "She said we could go to the beach together and that her family would make sure I felt right at home. I've only written to her a few times but it seems as if I've known her a long time."

"It's nice to feel so close to someone or something so far away," Aunt Sharon said.

"That's how I feel about you, Aunt Sharon," Ilana said, snuggling close to her again.

"That," Aunt Sharon nodded, holding Ilana tight, "is also how Jews have always felt about Israel."

No matter where we live, all Jews share a common bond: being Jewish and caring about one another.

כָּל-יִשְׂרָאֵל עֲרֵבִים זֶה לָזֶה.

Kol-yisrael arevim zeh lazeh.

12 ✡ Shavuot

Learning Is Not Just for School

Education

On Shavuot, the sixth and seventh of Sivan, Ilana and David like to stay up late for the *tikkun leil Shavuot*, an all-night study session on the first night that celebrates the Ten Commandments and the Torah. They enjoy a meal of blintzes, noodle puddings, cheese pastries, salads and fruit. They know that Shavuot is a "dairy holiday," since the Torah is described as "honey and milk under your tongue." Grandpa's super-duper fruit salad recalls the *bikkurim*, the first fruits that Jews from ancient Israel brought to Jerusalem to show their gratitude to God for the blessings they received every day.

When the Kedners go to synagogue on Shavuot, they hear the reading of the Ten Commandments as well as the Book of Ruth. Ilana listens carefully to the story of Ruth, a woman from Moab who shows her love and devotion to Naomi, her Israelite mother-in-law, as well as to the Jewish people. Ilana hopes that she, too, will become a proud and loyal Jewish leader.

"And a one and a two..." David faced the crowd in his grandparents' living room and lifted his hands like a conductor. "Please sing with us to the tune of *Yankee Doodle*," he announced.

David, Ilana, Michelle and Avi led the song they had made up for the holiday of Shavuot:

"Long ago in ancient times
the people stood at Sinai,
Moses went way up the mount
He almost touched the sky-yi.

The Torah gladly he received
Commandments one to ten,
To teach the people Yisrael
The kids, the women and men."

"Here's the chorus," Ilana said.

"Do not steal and do not kill,
Keep the Sabbath holy,

Honor both your mom and dad
And life will be good—totally!"

Everyone clapped. "Welcome to our *tikkun leil Shavuot*," Grandpa said. "On Shavuot we celebrate receiving the Ten Commandments and the Torah. That's why we've all gathered here to study tonight."

Ilana, Michelle and Avi sat down. David wanted to look around at everyone. It was best to be invisible for that. He squeezed himself into a small hiding space between the sofa and the grandfather clock.

The living room buzzed with people. David recognized Michelle's dad, Mr. Golden; Mrs. Friedman; Rabbi Aaron; and Uncle Morty, Grandpa's buddy with the mustache that curled down past his chin. Everyone was ready to stay up all night and study. Or at least until midnight. That was the Shavuot custom.

Earlier that morning, David had helped Grandma and Grandpa prepare for the *tikkun*. He had emptied nuts and raisins into bowls and polished the dining room table until it gleamed like the Torah's wooden handles. Grandma had cleaned the chandelier so it sparkled and filled a vase with roses from the garden. Grandpa had moved the furniture aside and arranged chairs in a semicircle.

But the preparations for the *tikkun* had started weeks before. Right after Pesach, Mom and Dad and their friends had discussed where to hold the *tikkun*. Mom had volunteered Grandma and Grandpa's house.

"That's a nice way of honoring your parents—by volunteering them for extra work!" Mr. Golden had joked.

"'Honor your father and mother' is one the Ten Commandments," Mom had laughed back.

"Why don't we study the Ten Commandments at the *tikkun*?" Dad had suggested. "Each family can learn about one of the commandments beforehand. Since we're so good at 'Honor your father and mother,' we'll take that one."

Now David listened as Grandpa introduced the discussion. "We've been counting the days since Pesach for this *tikkun*," he said. "It's been 49 days! Long ago the Israelites counted these same 49 days—called the *omer*—because it took 49 days for the wheat to be ready for harvesting. Let's see what wise thoughts have ripened in our minds."

"I've been counting the days until school ends," David piped up, no longer invisible.

"I think the Israelites had something else in mind," Grandpa chuckled.

"On Shavuot we thank God for pointing us in the right direction for a good life."

"God has a compass?" David asked.

"Yes," Uncle Morty nodded, twirling his mustache. "It's called the Ten Commandments."

David wrinkled his nose. "Do not do this. Do not do that. That's what I hear in school all the time."

"Aren't rules ever good?" Mrs. Friedman asked.

"If there weren't any rules," Avi said, "we could have spitball fights in the middle of class, and everyone could talk whenever they wanted. Nobody would learn."

"You need to know the rules to be a good baseball player," Rabbi Aaron said. "If you didn't know you had to touch home plate in order to score a run, you'd be out. The run wouldn't count."

"I guess without learning," David said slowly, "you can't become a good grownup either."

"The Torah has more than rules," Grandma said. "It shows us that God wants our help to make the world better."

"I know you guys are looking forward to camp," Mr. Golden said. "What if everyone picks on one of the kids in your group?"

"I know what that's like," Michelle said, with a hurt look on her face.

"I'd feel sorry for the kid, but I might be afraid not to go along with everyone," David answered. "They might pick on me too."

"We should care for everyone, the Torah says, no matter how difficult it might be," Mr. Golden said, glancing at Michelle.

Finally Grandpa invited all the guests into the dining room. The table overflowed with platters of cheese, cherry and blueberry blintzes, sweet noodle puddings, lasagne and baked ziti, and a hummus dip surrounded by carrot and celery sticks. The centerpiece was a huge assortment of fruit—apples and bananas, strawberries, canteloupe, watermelon, even papayas, mangoes and kiwi—fruit David had never even heard of until this morning. Another table held all kinds of cheesecakes.

"We chose an unusual variety of fruit," Grandpa explained, "so we can remember how the Jews in ancient Israel thanked God when the first fruit ripened on the trees. They went all the way to the Temple in Jerusalem with baskets of fruit called *bikkurim*."

Everyone took fruit. "*Barukh atah Adonai, Elohenu melekh ha'olam, borei pri ha'ets*," they recited together. "Praised are You, Adonai our God, who creates the fruit of the tree."

David ate until he thought he would pop like a balloon. He knew a treasure hunt for the kids was coming next. Grandma and Grandpa had hidden clues all over the house. As the kids found the answer to each clue, they would also find the letters that spelled the word "Shavuot."

David read the first clue out loud:

"This is as simple as apple pie
It's the first letter of the word 'Sinai'
You'll find this place before you can blink
Just climb upstairs to the bathroom..."

"...sink!" all the kids shouted, running upstairs. They found the letter "S" in a basket, with a chocolate chip cookie beside it.

"Grandma, you're the best!" David said, flinging his arms around her. "Mom is always telling me to treasure learning. She's always telling me that learning is not just for school. I think..." he paused to take a bite of the cookie, "I'm finally beginning to understand!"

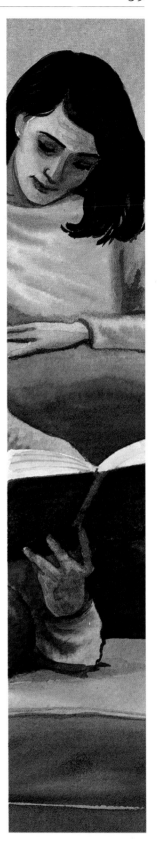

**Praised are You,
Adonai our God,
whose Torah guides us
wherever we go,
whatever we do,
for a good and Jewish life.**

בָּרוּךְ אַתָּה יְיָ, אֱלֹהֵינוּ מֶלֶךְ הָעוֹלָם,
אֲשֶׁר קִדְּשָׁנוּ בְּמִצְוֹתָיו וְצִוָּנוּ
לַעֲסוֹק בְּדִבְרֵי תוֹרָה.

Barukh atah Adonai, Elohenu melekh
ha'olam, asher kideshanu bemitsvotav
vetsivanu la'asok bedivrei torah.

13 ✡ Tisha B'Av
Creating Hope from Despair
Rebuilding

A fast day during the summer? Tisha B'Av is the one Jewish memorial day unfamiliar to Ilana and David. Mom and Dad explain that Tisha B'Av is the only other fast day besides Yom Kippur when Jews fast from sundown to sundown. For the first time, Ilana and David go with their parents to the evening Tisha B'Av service. Even though Tisha B'Av recalls the destruction of Jerusalem which took place long ago, everyone sits on low benches or on the floor as a sign of mourning, surrounded by candles. Mom and Dad help chant the biblical book of *Eikhah*, Lamentations, which describes how Jerusalem was destroyed and how the Jewish people were forced to leave Israel. People also read poems and rabbinic stories about the destruction of Jerusalem, and chant *kinnot*, dirges (mourning songs) written during the centuries when Jerusalem stood in ruins.

By the afternoon of Tisha B'Av, the mood changes from despair to hope, from destruction to rebuilding. Because Jerusalem was reunited in 1967, some friends of the Kedners fast only half a day, until the afternoon *Minchah* service. No matter what the practice, Tisha B'Av allows everyone a chance to think about the special place of Jerusalem in the life of the Jewish people.

"Frisky!" David cried. "How could you? My fortress is ruined! Mom! Dad! Come quickly."

Mom and Dad ran into David's room. "I was putting the last tower on my fortress," David sobbed. "I left the room for a minute, just to get a toothpick and a tissue to make a flag. When I came back, Frisky was in my room and blocks were everywhere!"

Mom hugged David. "I'm so sorry. I know you've been working on that fortress for days."

"I'll never be able to build such a good fortress again," David whimpered.

"It seems that way now," Mom consoled David. "But soon you'll feel like starting over. Maybe the new fortress will be even better."

"I don't know how to start rebuilding," David said. "It's too hard to do all by myself."

"We'll help," Dad said.

"I'm pretty good at towers and moats," said Ilana, who had wandered in.

"Okay," David nodded. "But it's still going to be tough."

"That reminds me of a story," Dad said. "A true story. A long time ago the Jewish people built a magnificent Temple in Jerusalem. They called it the *Bet Ha-mikdash.*"

"Did it have lots of towers?" David asked.

"It had a big wall around it and gates made of stone," Dad replied. "It had carvings of angels and lions, a golden altar and lamps. Three times a year Jews from other cities and countries came to Jerusalem to celebrate Pesach, Shavuot and Sukkot. Those were joyous, festive times."

"I'll be the lion," David said. He climbed on a chair and roared.

"Good. You left the angel part for me," Ilana said.

"Now comes the sad chapter of the story," Dad said. "Our enemies destroyed the Temple. For many years, it remained desolate, until the people could rebuild it. Believe it or not, after it was rebuilt it was destroyed again, and the city of Jerusalem along with it. Most of the Jews were forced to leave."

"But cousin Gideon lives there now," David said.

"The city was rebuilt in modern times," Dad replied, "but the Temple was never rebuilt. The only piece of it that remained standing was the Western Wall, the Kotel."

"In school we wrote little wishes to put in the cracks of the Kotel," Ilana interrupted. "Mrs. Geffen took them with her when she visited her family in Jerusalem."

"What did you wish for?" David asked.

"It's private. It's between me and God," Ilana answered.

"The Kotel is stuffed with notes," Mom said. "People feel God's presence there."

"Even though we can pray at the Kotel now, we still remember the destruction of the Temple on a fast day called Tisha B'Av, the ninth day of the month of Av. It so happens that Tisha B'Av is next week," Dad said.

"I've never heard of Tisha B'Av," Ilana said. "I thought I knew all the holidays."

"That's probably because Tisha B'Av always falls in July or August," Mom explained, "so you don't learn about it in school."

"You could have told us about it," Ilana said.

"We thought it was such a sad holiday that you wouldn't be interested," Mom answered. "Maybe we were wrong."

"Do we spend all day in synagogue like we do on Yom Kippur?" Ilana asked.

"No," Mom assured her. "At night and in the morning, we read a book of the Bible, *Eikhah*, that mourns the destruction of Jerusalem. After the morning service, you can do all kinds of special projects. I remember when I went to camp, we rebound old, damaged Jewish books. It was our way of showing we could also rebuild."

"There are so many sad things in the world today," Ilana said. "Why cry over what happened so long ago?"

Dad took a puzzle off David's shelf. "A piece of this puzzle is lost," he said. "When Jerusalem was destroyed, Judaism became like a puzzle with a missing piece. We had holidays to celebrate, and customs and laws to follow, but we missed an important piece of our identity—Jerusalem."

"Without Jerusalem, Judaism wasn't complete?" Ilana asked. "How did Jews survive?"

"It was hard," Dad nodded. "For 2,000 years—can you imagine?—Jews all over the world remembered Jerusalem in their songs and prayers. They longed to return and rebuild it. But they had no choice. To replace the Temple, they built synagogues wherever they lived."

David tinkered with his blocks. "How was Jerusalem rebuilt?"

"Until 1967, Jerusalem was a divided city," Mom replied. "Part of it was in Israel and part of it was in another country named Jordan. Many of the synagogues and Jewish neighborhoods were destroyed. Then the Israeli army recaptured all of Jerusalem during an amazing war which only lasted six days."

"I wish I had been there!" David whistled.

"It was unbelievably quick and exciting," Dad admitted, "but many soldiers died in the battle for Jerusalem. When the Israeli army reached the Kotel, the soldiers cried."

"Soldiers don't cry," David scoffed.

"They weren't tears of sadness," Dad replied. "They had done what Jews had dreamed of for 2,000 years. Their parents had talked about it. Their grandparents had yearned for it. But they were the ones who made Jerusalem one city again."

"Did they rebuild the synagogues?" Ilana asked.

"Yes," Mom nodded. "And Jewish homes, shops, streets, restaurants and playgrounds."

"You see, David?" Dad said. "Sometimes rebuilding takes a long time, but it's worth the wait."

"I don't want to wait anymore," David said eagerly. "Let's start rebuilding right now!"

As David formed squares of blocks, Mom kneeled down and added triangular turrets and arched gates. Dad and Ilana built a solid outside wall with towers on four sides, which David decorated with colorful flags. Soon a new fortress emerged, strong and majestic, like the city of Jerusalem itself.

**Praised are You,
Adonai our God,
who consoles Israel
and rebuilds Jerusalem.**

בָּרוּךְ אַתָּה יְיָ, אֱלֹהֵינוּ מֶלֶךְ הָעוֹלָם,
מְנַחֵם צִיּוֹן וּבוֹנֵה יְרוּשָׁלָיִם.

Barukh atah Adonai, Elohenu melekh ha'olam,
menachem tsiyon uvoneh yerushalayim.